T0284148

POEMS ON NATURE

POEMS ON NATURE

With an introduction by
HELEN MACDONALD

Selection and arrangement by
GABY MORGAN

MACMILLAN COLLECTOR'S LIBRARY

This collection first published 2019 by Macmillan Collector's Library

This edition first published 2024 by Macmillan Collector's Library
an imprint of Pan Macmillan
The Smithson, 6 Briset Street, London, ECIM 5NR
EU representative: Macmillan Publishers Ireland Ltd, 1st Floor,
The Liffey Trust Centre, 117-126 Sheriff Street Upper,
Dublin 1, DO1 YC43
Associated companies throughout the world
www.panmacmillan.com

ISBN 978-1-0350-2676-0

Selection and arrangement © Macmillan Publishers International Ltd 2019
Introduction © Helen Macdonald 2019

1 3 5 7 9 8 6 4 2

A CIP catalogue record for this book is available from the British Library.

Cover and endpaper design: Daisy Bates, Pan Macmillan Art Department
Typeset in Plantin MT Std by Jouve (UK), Milton Keynes
Printed and bound in China by Imago

Visit **www.panmacmillan.com** to read more about all our books
and to buy them. You will also find features, author interviews and
news of any author events, and you can sign up for e-newsletters
so that you're always first to hear about our new releases.

Contents

SUMMER

AUTUMN

WINTER

Introduction

HELEN MACDONALD

I wrote my first poem when I was six years old. It was an ode to a dandelion. I remember nothing about it except that it rhymed 'golden flower' with 'fairy bower'. I'm sure it was a very bad poem, but it was interesting all the same, because even at that early age I'd assumed the right way to write about nature was with a poem. There are numerous right ways to write about the natural world, from ecological research papers to long-form journalism, but I've come to think that nature poems are among the most fascinating human responses to the wildlife and landscapes around us. They're a rich and complex tradition, and far from simple responses to the natural world. Poems on nature reflect not only our changing relationship with the natural environment, but human culture, society, politics, war, trauma and con-temporary understandings of selfhood. In whatever age they were composed, nature poems are always, at heart, expressions of human concerns. Perhaps the most poignant of all are those which are bound up, often invisibly, with terrible events. Edward Thomas's poems of the English countryside were written during the horror of the Great War, and John Clare's poems were composed at a time when the Enclosure Act was remorselessly destroying the traditional fabric of rural life.

This anthology focuses on work from Britain, Ireland and America, temperate lands where seasons mark the passage of time. The poems range from traditional

Northumbrian farming rhymes to the songs and sonnets of Shakespeare, rich meditative poems of the Romantics, the compressed, luminous poems of Emily Dickinson, in which the observation of nature becomes a means to grapple with far deeper meanings, to the verses of Georgian poets for whom an attic of stored apples becomes a near-mystical scene, ripe for meditation.

Nature is a phenomenally difficult concept to define, and these poems express its various meanings. For some, nature speaks of home and community, for others it is a place for solitary introspection. It can be a cruel and impassive force or a benevolent one; sometimes remote, other times familiar, even liable to give revelations of divine power. Sometimes the nature in these poems seems indivisible from our own human nature; in others it's something entirely separate from us and all our concerns. The best nature poetry, I think, exists in the space between those two positions, trying to understand our connection with the world around us. And very often, nature is presented in these poems as a corrective to the mores and trials of modern life, a green refuge when that world is too much with us.

Two ancient works, Theocritus' Idylls, and Virgil's Eclogues, were the foundational texts of the pastoral tradition in poetry. They celebrated an idealized rural landscape inhabited by shepherds, a place of simplicity far from the frenetic, complicated life of towns and cities. Over the centuries, the pastoral was shaped, elaborated, copied and reworked, and become a model for writing about the relationship between nature and artifice in worlds closer to home, and in restricted landscapes, too, such as in the gloriously complex garden poems of Andrew Marvell. By the eighteenth century, the pastoral was still being written, but had become increasingly self-conscious and ripe for parody. It saw a later resurgence in Victorian poetry in the form of pastoral elegies.

Nature underwent an intellectual remaking by the Romantics at the end of the eighteenth and the beginning of the nineteenth centuries. The poems of Wordsworth and Coleridge show us a nature that is a benevolent, comforting power; it brings joy and fosters wisdom in the virtuous heart. The Romantics considered estrangement from nature to be the root of many of mankind's ills. It is a conception of nature that has been highly influential. The legacy of the Romantics can be found in many later traditions, including that of the American transcendentalists, who shared the Romantics' sense of the mystical power of nature. They saw unity in all things: Walt Whitman maintained that nature itself was the only complete and actual poem.

Nature poems aren't all verdant landscapes, forest pastures, and wild mountaintops. There are many creatures in these pages, ranging from hares to turkeys, moths, caterpillars, chaffinches and mice. Some species appear repeatedly, and have accrued a weight of poetic symbolism over the centuries. It's hard to hear a live, singing nightingale without recalling its place in the poetic tradition, for its literary meanings have become entwined with our perception of the real bird. In some poems, animals seem little more than motifs or metaphors, but in others, they are portrayed in ways that break free of poetic convention to become thrillingly alive, as with the birds in the poems of John Clare. He had an astonishing capacity for acute observation and a deep familiarity with his local wildlife; his poems remind us that nature is always far more than a repository for human meaning. Perhaps the most delightful individual animal here is a wild creature raised in a domesticated setting. 'Old Tiney', John Cowper's hare, is vividly, brightly present; we're shown him nibbling carrots, leaping about a Turkish carpet, and taking bread from Cowper's hand, though never without a tendency to bite.

In some poems, animal, poet and history exquisitely coincide, as with Thomas Hardy's darkling thrush carolling in a desolate landscape, offering hope to the poet right at the beginning of a new century. But there are good reasons to write generic creatures rather than individual ones into a poem. They can offer the poet a vision of eternity. While individual creatures die, they are replaced by progeny that exactly resemble them, and thus they are always somehow present, unchanged. The cuckoos of 'Sumer is i-cumin in' are, in this sense, the same cuckoos that John Clare watched in his Northamptonshire village, and the same cuckoos that fly and call today. The notion that the countryside is a place of eternal, unchanging richness is eloquently expressed in poems written by those far from home, in which the imagined rural landscape of one's home country becomes a mental refuge from exile and difficult circumstances; indeed, the nature of home can be a highly-charged, problematic notion in works written in the age of Empire.

The relationship between time, human life, and the natural world is a central concern in much nature poetry. Although the countryside seems eternal, its altering seasons are a ready metaphor for changes in human lives and fortunes. The blooming and dying of flowers, for example, can be a vivid reminder of the inexorable passage of time. 'There is no life like Spring-life born to die', wrote Christina Rossetti. In a related way, works in which the poet regards the natural world late in their life, as in A. E. Housman's poem 'Loveliest of trees, the cherry now', show how natural beauty can seem brighter and more meaningful while harder to bear in the face of the brute fact of human mortality. But there are poems of nature here that are far from deep meditations on life and death: comic works, like Thomas Hood's 'No!' and Rupert Brooke's 'Heaven'. Paul Laurence Dunbar's 'Signs of the Times', is droll and delightful – though it's significant that despite being an accomplished traditional poet, he found it difficult to publish anything other than comedic poems written in African-American Vernacular English.

Along with their literary significance and beauty, the poems collected in this anthology give the reader insight into our changing assumptions about nature over the centuries. And at this current historical moment, they can be read as something else: a warning. We have now come to realize that the riches of the landscapes around us are not eternal. The rapid decline in biodiversity since the nineteenth century, and particularly since the 1970s, through industrialization, development, pollution, intensive farming, pesticides and climate change make many of these poems read like monuments to what we have lost and are still losing. For a seventeenth-century poet, the English landscape in spring would have been loud with the rich song of nightingales, the call of the cuckoo. These would have seemed as unremarkable and predictable a feature of life as summer warmth and winter cold. Even in my childhood, I expected to hear cuckoos whenever I walked in fields. Now nightingales and cuckoos have become so rare that many people, even those living in rural areas, never hear them. The corncrake, the land-rail whose call Edward Thomas wrote of as a ubiquitous summer sound 'heard in every vale' is practically absent from the British mainland. It's sobering to think that we are not only losing the creatures around us, but we might be heading towards a time when the things in nature poetry cannot mean anything to us any more, for they are gone. This anthology, with all its riches, is a reminder that the loss of nature's riches does not simply diminish just the world, but our art and minds and hearts as well.

POEMS ON NATURE

SPRING

'The year's at the spring'

The year's at the spring
And day's at the morn;
Morning's at seven;
The hillside's dew-pearled;
The lark's on the wing;
The snail's on the thorn:
God's in His heaven—
All's right with the world!

Robert Browning
(1812–1889)

I so liked Spring

I so liked Spring last year
    Because you were here;–
        The thrushes too–
Because it was these you so liked to hear–
        I so liked you.

    This year's a different thing,–
        I'll not think of you.
But I'll like Spring because it is simply Spring
        As the thrushes do.

Charlotte Mew (1869–1928)

There Will Come Soft Rains

There will come soft rains and the smell of the
   ground,
And swallows circling with their shimmering sound;

And frogs in the pools, singing at night,
And wild plum trees in tremulous white,

Robins will wear their feathery fire,
Whistling their whims on a low fence-wire;

And not one will know of the war, not one
Will care at last when it is done.

Not one would mind, neither bird nor tree,
If mankind perished utterly;

And Spring herself, when she woke at dawn,
Would scarcely know that we were gone.

Sara Teasdale (1884–1933)

To a Snowdrop

Lone Flower, hemmed in with snows and white as they
But hardier far, once more I see thee bend
Thy forehead, as if fearful to offend,
Like an unbidden guest. Though day by day,
Storms, sallying from the mountain-tops, waylay
The rising sun, and on the plains descend;
Yet art thou welcome, welcome as a friend
Whose zeal outruns his promise! Blue-eyed May
Shall soon behold this border thickly set
With bright jonquils, their odours lavishing
On the soft west-wind and his frolic peers;
Nor will I then thy modest grace forget,
Chaste Snowdrop, venturous harbinger of Spring,
And pensive monitor of fleeting years!

William Wordsworth (1770–1850)

February Twilight

I stood beside a hill
      Smooth with new-laid snow,
A single star looked out
      From the cold evening glow.

There was no other creature
      That saw what I could see –
I stood and watched the evening star
      As long as it watched me.

Sara Teasdale (1884–1933)

Spring

Sound the Flute!
      Now it's mute.
      Birds delight
      Day and Night;
      Nightingale
      In the dale
      Lark in Sky,
      Merrily,
Merrily, Merrily, to welcome in the Year.

      Little Boy,
      Full of joy;
      Little Girl,
      Sweet and small;
      Cock does crow,
      So do you;
      Merry voice,
      Infant noise,
Merrily, Merrily, to welcome in the Year.

      Little Lamb,
      Here I am;
      Come and lick
      My white neck;
      Let me pull
      Your soft Wool;
      Let me kiss
      Your soft face:
Merrily, Merrily, we welcome in the Year.

William Blake (1757–1827)

Thaw

Over the land freckled with snow half-thawed
The speculating rooks at their nests cawed
And saw from elm-tops, delicate as flower of grass,
What we below could not see, Winter pass.

Edward Thomas (1878–1917)

Spring

Frost-locked all the winter,
Seeds, and roots, and stones of fruits,
What shall make their sap ascend
That they may put forth shoots?
Tips of tender green,
Leaf, or blade, or sheath;
Telling of the hidden life
That breaks forth underneath,
Life nursed in its grave by Death.

Blows the thaw-wind pleasantly,
Drips the soaking rain,
By fits looks down the waking sun:
Young grass springs on the plain;
Young leaves clothe early hedgerow trees;
Seeds, and roots, and stones of fruits,
Swollen with sap put forth their shoots;
Curled-headed ferns sprout in the lane;
Birds sing and pair again.

There is no time like Spring,
When life's alive in everything,
Before new nestlings sing,
Before cleft swallows speed their journey back
Along the trackless track –
God guides their wing,
He spreads their table that they nothing lack, –
Before the daisy grows a common flower
Before the sun has power
To scorch the world up in his noontide hour.

There is no time like Spring,
Like Spring that passes by;
There is no life like Spring-life born to die,
Piercing the sod,
Clothing the uncouth clod,
Hatched in the nest,
Fledged on the windy bough,
Strong on the wing:
There is no time like Spring that passes by,
Now newly born, and now
Hastening to die.

Christina Rossetti (1830–1894)

Her Anxiety

Earth in beauty dressed
Awaits returning spring.
All true love must die,
Alter at the best
Into some lesser thing.
Prove that I lie.

Such body lovers have.
Such exacting breath,
That they touch or sigh.
Every touch they give,
Love is nearer death.
Prove that I lie.

W. B. Yeats (1865–1939)

Invitation to the Country

Now 'tis Spring on wood and wold,
Early Spring that shivers with cold,
But gladdens, and gathers, day by day,
A lovelier hue, a warmer ray,
A sweeter song, a dearer ditty;
Ouzel and throstle, new-mated and gay,
Singing their bridals on every spray–
Oh, hear them, deep in the songless City!
Cast off the yoke of toil and smoke,
As Spring is casting winter's grey,
As serpents cast their skins away:
And come, for the Country awaits thee with pity
And longs to bathe thee in her delight,
And take a new joy in thy kindling sight;
And I no less, by day and night,
Long for thy coming, and watch for, and wait thee,
And wonder what duties can thus belate thee.

Dry-fruited firs are dropping their cones,
And vista'd avenues of pines
Take richer green, give fresher tones,
As morn after morn the glad sun shines.

Primrose tufts peep over the brooks,
Fair faces amid moist decay!
The rivulets run with the dead leaves at play,
The leafless elms are alive with the rooks.

Over the meadows the cowslips are springing,
The marshes are thick with king-cup gold,
Clear is the cry of the lambs in the fold,
The skylark is singing, and singing, and singing.

Soon comes the cuckoo when April is fair,
And her blue eye the brighter the more it may weep:
The frog and the butterfly wake from their sleep,
Each to its element, water and air.

Mist hangs still on every hill,
And curls up the valleys at eve; but noon
Is fullest of Spring; and at midnight the moon
Gives her westering throne to Orion's bright zone,
As he slopes o'er the darkened world's repose;
And a lustre in eastern Sirius glows.

Come, in the season of opening buds;
Come, and molest not the otter that whistles
Unlit by the moon, 'mid the wet winter bristles
Of willow, half-drowned in the fattening floods.
Let him catch his cold fish without fear of a gun,
And the stars shall shield him, and thou wilt shun!
And every little bird under the sun
Shall know that the bounty of Spring doth dwell
In the winds that blow, in the waters that run,
And in the breast of man as well.

George Meredith (1828–1909)

To my Sister

It is the first mild day of March:
Each minute sweeter than before,
The red-breast sings from the tall larch
That stands beside our door.

There is a blessing in the air,
Which seems a sense of joy to yield
To the bare trees, and mountains bare,
And grass in the green field.

My Sister! ('tis a wish of mine)
Now that our morning meal is done,
Make haste, your morning task resign;
Come forth and feel the sun.

Edward will come with you – and, pray,
Put on with speed your woodland dress,
And bring no book: for this one day
We'll give to idleness.

No joyless forms shall regulate
Our living Calendar:
We from today, my friend, will date
The opening of the year.

Love, now an universal birth,
From heart to heart is stealing,
From earth to man, from man to earth –
It is the hour of feeling.

One moment now may give us more
Than fifty years of reason;
Our minds shall drink at every pore
The spirit of the season.

Some silent laws our hearts will make,
Which they shall long obey:
We for the year to come may take
Our temper from today.

And from the blessed power that rolls
About, below, above,
We'll frame the measure of our souls:
They shall be tuned to love.

Then come, my sister! come, I pray,
With speed put on your woodland dress,
And bring no book: for this one day
We'll give to idleness.

William Wordsworth (1770–1850)

'Dear March – Come In –'

Dear March – Come In –
How glad I am –
I hoped for you before –
Put down your Hat –
You must have walked –
How out of Breath you are –
Dear March, how are you, and the Rest –
Did you leave Nature well –
Oh March, Come right up stairs with me –
I have so much to tell –

I got your Letter, and the Birds –
The Maples never knew that you were
    coming – till I called
I declare – how Red their Faces grew –
But March, forgive me – and
All those Hills you left for me to Hue –
There was no Purple suitable –
You took it all with you –

Who knocks? That April.
Lock the Door –
I will not be pursued –
He stayed away a Year to call
When I am occupied –
But trifles look so trivial
As soon as you have come

That Blame is just as dear as Praise
And Praise as mere as Blame –

Emily Dickinson (1830–1886)

The Lamb

Little Lamb, who made thee?
  Dost thou know who made thee?
Gave thee life, and bid thee feed
By the stream and o'er the mead;
Gave thee clothing of delight,
Softest clothing, woolly, bright;
Gave thee such a tender voice,
Making all the vales rejoice?
  Little Lamb, who made thee?
  Dost thou know who made thee?

Little Lamb, I'll tell thee,
  Little Lamb, I'll tell thee:
He is callèd by thy name,
For He calls himself a Lamb.
He is meek, and He is mild;
He became a little child.
I, a child, and thou a lamb,
We are callèd by His name.
  Little Lamb, God bless thee!
  Little Lamb, God bless thee!

William Blake (1757–1827)

March

March yeans the lammie
  And buds the thorn,
And blows through the flint
  Of an ox's horn.

Anon.

I Wandered Lonely as a Cloud

I wandered lonely as a cloud
That floats on high o'er vales and hills,
When all at once I saw a crowd,
A host, of golden daffodils;
Beside the lake, beneath the trees,
Fluttering and dancing in the breeze.

Continuous as the stars that shine
And twinkle on the milky way,
They stretched in never-ending line
Along the margin of a bay:
Ten thousand saw I at a glance,
Tossing their heads in sprightly dance.

The waves beside them danced; but they
Out-did the sparkling waves in glee:
A poet could not but be gay,
In such a jocund company:
I gazed—and gazed—but little thought
What wealth the show to me had brought:

For oft, when on my couch I lie
In vacant or in pensive mood,
They flash upon that inward eye
Which is the bliss of solitude;
And then my heart with pleasure fills,
And dances with the daffodils.

William Wordsworth (1770–1850)

To Daffodils

Fair daffodils, we weep to see
  You haste away so soon;
As yet the early-rising sun
  Has not attain'd his noon.
     Stay, stay,
  Until the hasting day
      Has run
  But to the evensong;
And, having prayed together, we
  Will go with you along.

We have short time to stay, as you,
  We have as short a spring;
As quick a growth to meet decay,
  As you, or anything.
     We die,
  As your hours do, and dry
      Away,
  Like to the summer's rain;
Or as the pearls of morning's dew,
  Ne'er to be found again.

Robert Herrick (1591–1674)

Mothering Sunday

It is the day of all the year,
Of all the year the one day,
When I shall see my Mother dear
   And bring her cheer,
A-Mothering on Sunday.

And now to fetch my wheaten cake,
To fetch it from the baker,
He promised me, for Mother's sake,
   The best he'd bake
For me to fetch and take her.

Well have I known, as I went by
One hollow lane, that none day
I'd fail to find – for all they're shy –
   Where violets lie,
As I went home on Sunday.

My sister Jane is waiting-maid
Along with Squire's lady;
And year by year her part she's played,
   And home she stayed
To get the dinner ready.

For Mother'll come to Church, you'll see –
Of all the year it's the day –
'The one,' she'll say, 'that's made for me.'
   And so it be:
It's every Mother's free day.

The boys will all come home from town,
Not one will miss that one day;
And every maid will bustle down
  To show her gown,
A-Mothering on Sunday.

It is the day of all the year,
Of all the year the one day;
And here come I, my Mother dear,
  And bring you cheer,
A-Mothering on Sunday.

George Hare Leonard (1863–1941)

I Watched a Blackbird

I watched a blackbird on a budding sycamore
One Easter Day, when sap was stirring twigs
   to the core;
I saw his tongue, and crocus-coloured bill
Parting and closing as he turned his trill;
Then he flew down seized on a stem of hay,
And upped to where his building scheme
   was under way,
As if so sure a nest were never shaped on spray.

Thomas Hardy (1840–1928)

Loveliest of trees

Loveliest of trees, the cherry now
Is hung with bloom along the bough,
And stands about the woodland ride
Wearing white for Eastertide.

Now, of my threescore years and ten,
Twenty will not come again,
And take from seventy springs a score,
It only leaves me fifty more.

And since to look at things in bloom
Fifty springs are little room,
About the woodlands I will go
To see the cherry hung with snow.

A. E. Housman (1859–1936)

The Cuckoo

In April
Come he will,
In flow'ry May
He sings all day,
In leafy June
He changes his tune,
In bright July
He's ready to fly,
In August
Go he must.

Anon.

The Cuckoo

O the cuckoo she's a pretty bird,
   She singeth as she flies,
She bringeth good tidings,
   She telleth no lies.

She sucketh white flowers,
   For to keep her voice clear,
And the more she singeth cuckoo,
   The summer draweth near.

Anon.

The Woods and Banks

The woods and banks of England now,
   Late coppered with dead leaves and old,
Have made the early violets grow,
   And bulge with knots of primrose gold.
Hear how the blackbird flutes away,
   Whose music scorns to sleep at night:
Hear how the cuckoo shouts all day
   For echoes – to the world's delight:
Hullo, you imp of wonder, you –
   Where are you now, cuckoo? Cuckoo?

W. H. Davies (1871–1940)

Little Trotty Wagtail

Little trotty wagtail, he went in the rain,
And tittering, tottering sideways he ne'er got straight
   again.
He stooped to get a worm, and look'd up to catch a
   fly,
And then he flew away ere his feathers they were dry.

Little trotty wagtail, he waddled in the mud,
And left his little footmarks, trample where he would.
He waddled in the water-pudge, and waggle went his
   tail,
And he chirrup up his wings to dry upon the garden
   rail.

Little trotty wagtail, you nimble all about,
And in the dimpling water-pudge you waddle in and
   out;
Your home is nigh at hand, and in the warm pigsty,
So, little Master Wagtail, I'll bid you a goodbye.

John Clare (1793–1864)

Home Thoughts from Abroad

Oh, to be in England
Now that April's there,
And whoever wakes in England
Sees, some morning, unaware,
That the lowest boughs and the brushwood sheaf
Round the elm-tree bole are in tiny leaf,
While the chaffinch sings on the orchard bough
In England – now!
And after April, when May follows,
And the whitethroat builds, and all the swallows!
Hark, where my blossomed pear-tree in the hedge
Leans to the field and scatters on the clover
Blossoms and dewdrops – at the bent spray's edge –
That's the wise thrush; he sings each song twice over,
Lest you should think he never could recapture
The first fine careless rapture!
And though the fields look rough with hoary dew,
All will be gay when noontide wakes anew
The buttercups, the little children's dower
– Far brighter than this gaudy melon-flower.

Robert Browning (1812–1889)

On a Lane in Spring

A little lane – the brook runs close beside,
  And spangles in the sunshine, while the fish
    glide swiftly by;
And hedges leafing with the green springtide;
  From out their greenery the old birds fly,
And chirp and whistle in the morning sun;
  The pilewort glitters 'neath the pale blue sky,
The little robin has its nest begun
  The grass-green linnets round the bushes fly.
How mild the spring comes in! the daisy buds
  Lift up their golden blossoms to the sky.
  How lovely are the pingles and the woods!
  Here a beetle runs – and there a fly
Rests on the arum leaf in bottle-green,
And all the spring in this sweet lane is seen.

John Clare (1793–1864)

Spring

Nothing is so beautiful as Spring –
   When weeds, in wheels, shoot long and lovely and
     lush;
   Thrush's eggs look little low heavens, and thrush
Through the echoing timber does so rinse and wring
The ear, it strikes like lightnings to hear him sing;
   The glassy peartree leaves and blooms, they brush
   The descending blue; that blue is all in a rush
With richness; the racing lambs too have fair their
     fling.

What is all this juice and all this joy?
   A strain of the earth's sweet being in the
     beginning
In Eden garden. – Have, get, before it cloy,
   Before it cloud, Christ, lord, and sour with sinning,
Innocent mind and Mayday in girl and boy,
   Most, O maid's child, thy choice and worthy the
     winning.

Gerard Manley Hopkins (1844–1889)

The Starlight Night

Look at the stars! look, look up at the skies!
  O look at all the fire-folk sitting in the air!
  The bright boroughs, the circle-citadels there!
Down in dim woods the diamond delves! the
    elves'-eyes!
The grey lawns cold where gold, where quickgold lies!
  Wind-beat whitebeam! airy abeles set on a flare!
  Flake-doves sent floating forth at a farmyard scare!
Ah well! it is all a purchase, all is a prize.

Buy then! bid then! – What? – Prayer, patience, alms,
    vows.
Look, look: a May-mess, like on orchard boughs!
  Look! March-bloom, like on mealed-with-yellow
    sallows!
These are indeed the barn; withindoors house
The shocks. This piece-bright paling shuts the spouse
  Christ home, Christ and his mother and all his
    hallows.

Gerard Manley Hopkins (1844–1889)

Tall Nettles

Tall nettles cover up, as they have done
  These many springs, the rusty harrow, the
    plough
Long worn out, and the roller made of stone;
  Only the elm butt tops the nettles now.

This corner of the farmyard I like most:
  As well as any bloom upon a flower
I like the dust on the nettles, never lost
  Except to prove the sweetness of a shower.

Edward Thomas (1878–1917)

'When that I was and a little tiny boy'

When that I was and a little tiny boy,
  With hey, ho, the wind and the rain;
A foolish thing was but a toy,
  For the rain it raineth every day.

But when I came to man's estate,
  With hey, ho, the wind and the rain;
'Gainst knaves and thieves men shut their gates,
  For the rain it raineth every day.

But when I came, alas! to wive,
  With hey, ho, the wind and the rain;
By swaggering could I never thrive,
  For the rain it raineth every day.

But when I came unto my beds,
  With hey, ho, the wind and the rain;
With toss-pots still had drunken heads,
  For the rain it raineth every day.

A great while ago the world begun,
  With hey, ho, the wind and the rain;
But that's all one, our play is done,
  And we strive to please you every day.

William Shakespeare (1564–1616)

Sonnet 98

From you have I been absent in the spring,
When proud-pied April, dress'd in all his trim,
Hath put a spirit of youth in everything,
That heavy Saturn laugh'd, and leap'd with him.
Yet nor the lays of birds, nor the sweet smell
Of different flowers in odour and in hue,
Could make me any summer's story tell,
Or from their proud lap pluck them where they grew:
Nor did I wonder at the lily's white,
Nor praise the deep vermilion in the rose;
They were but sweet, but figures of delight,
Drawn after you – you pattern of all those.
   Yet seem'd it winter still, and, you away,
   As with your shadow I with these did play.

William Shakespeare (1564–1616)

But These Things Also

But these things also are Spring's—
On banks by the roadside the grass
Long-dead that is greyer now
Than all the Winter it was;

The shell of a little snail bleached
In the grass; chip of flint, and mite
Of chalk; and the small birds' dung
In splashes of purest white:

All the white things a man mistakes
For earliest violets
Who seeks through Winter's ruins
Something to pay Winter's debts,

While the North blows, and starling flocks
By chattering on and on
Keep their spirits up in the mist,
And Spring's here, Winter's not gone.

Edward Thomas (1878–1917)

The Argument of His Book

I sing of brooks, of blossoms, birds, and bowers,
Of April, May, of June, and July flowers.
I sing of May-poles, hock-carts, wassails, wakes,
Of bridegrooms, brides, and of their bridal-cakes.
I write of youth, of love, and have access
By these to sing of cleanly wantonness.
I sing of dews, of rains, and piece by piece
Of balm, of oil, of spice, and ambergris.
I sing of Time's trans-shifting; and I write
How roses first came red, and lilies white.
I write of groves, of twilights, and I sing
The court of Mab, and of the fairy king.
I write of Hell; I sing (and ever shall)
Of Heaven, and hope to have it after all.

Robert Herrick (1591–1674)

The Song of Wandering Aengus

I went out to the hazel wood,
Because a fire was in my head,
And cut and peeled a hazel wand,
And hooked a berry to a thread;
And when white moths were on the wing,
And moth-like stars were flickering out,
I dropped the berry in a stream
And caught a little silver trout.

When I had laid it on the floor
I went to blow the fire aflame,
But something rustled on the floor,
And someone called me by my name;
It had become a glimmering girl
With apple blossom in her hair
Who called me by my name and ran
And faded through the brightening air.

Though I am old with wandering
Through hollow lands and hilly lands,
I will find out where she has gone,
And kiss her lips and take her hands;
And walk among long dappled grass,
And pluck till time and times are done,
The silver apples of the moon,
The golden apples of the sun.

W. B. Yeats (1865–1939)

A Brilliant Day

O keen pellucid air! nothing can lurk
Or disavow itself on this bright day;
The small rain-plashes shine from far away,
The tiny emmet glitters at his work;
The bee looks blithe and gay, and as she plies
Her task, and moves and sidles round the cup
Of this spring flower, to drink its honey up,
Her glassy wings, like oars that dip and rise,
Gleam momently. Pure-bosom'd, clear of fog,
The long lake glistens, while the glorious beam
Bespangles the wet joints and floating leaves
Of water-plants, whose every point receives
His light; and jellies of the spawning frog,
Unmark'd before, like piles of jewels seem!

Charles Tennyson Turner (1808–1879)

SUMMER

Summer

Winter is cold-hearted,
  Spring is yea and nay,
Autumn is a weathercock
  Blown every way:
Summer days for me
  When every leaf is on its tree;

When Robin's not a beggar,
  And Jenny Wren's a bride,
And larks hang singing, singing, singing,
  Over the wheat-fields wide,
  And anchored lilies ride,
And the pendulum spider
  Swings from side to side,

And blue-black beetles transact business,
  And gnats fly in a host,
And furry caterpillars hasten
  That no time be lost,
And moths grow fat and thrive,
And ladybirds arrive.

Before green apples blush,
  Before green nuts embrown,
Why, one day in the country
  Is worth a month in town;
  Is worth a day and a year
Of the dusty, musty, lag-last fashion
  That days drone elsewhere.

Christina Rossetti (1830–1894)

The Happy Countryman

Who can live in heart so glad
As the merry country lad?
Who upon a fair green balk
May at pleasure sit and walk,
And amid the azure skies
See the morning sun arise, –
While he hears in every spring
How the birds do chirp and sing:
Or before the hounds in cry
See the hare go stealing by:
Or along the shallow brook,
Angling with a baited hook,
See the fishes leap and play
In a blessèd sunny day:
Or to hear the partridge call,
Till she have her covey all:
Or to see the subtle fox,
How the villain plies the box:
After feeding on his prey,
How he closely sneaks away,
Through the hedge and down the furrow
Till he gets into his burrow:
Then the bee to gather honey,
And the little black-haired coney,
On a bank for sunny place,
With her forefeet wash her face:
Are not these, with thousand moe
Than the courts of kings do know,
The true pleasing spirit's sights
That may breed true love's delights? . . .

Nicholas Breton (1545–1626)

A Day

I'll tell you how the sun rose,—
A ribbon at a time.
The steeples swam in amethyst,
The news like squirrels ran.

The hills untied their bonnets,
The bobolinks begun.
Then I said softly to myself,
"That must have been the sun!"

But how he set, I know not.
There seemed a purple stile
Which little yellow boys and girls
Were climbing all the while

Till when they reached the other side,
A dominie in gray
Put gently up the evening bars,
And led the flock away.

Emily Dickinson (1830–1886)

My Hearts Leaps Up

My heart leaps up when I behold
   A rainbow in the sky:
So was it when my life began;
So is it now I am a man;
So be it when I shall grow old,
   Or let me die!
The Child is father of the Man;
And I could wish my days to be
Bound each to each by natural piety.

William Wordsworth (1770–1850)

The Merry Month of May

O! the month of May, the merry month of May,
　So frolic, so gay, and so green, so green, so green!
O! and then did I unto my true Love say,
　Sweet Peg, thou shalt be my Summer's Queen.

Now the nightingale, the pretty nightingale,
　The sweetest singer in all the forest choir,
Entreats thee, sweet Peggy, to hear thy true love's tale:
　Lo! yonder she sitteth, her breast against a briar.

But O! I spy the cuckoo, the cuckoo, the cuckoo;
　See where she sitteth; come away, my joy:
Come away, I prithee, I do not like the cuckoo
　Should sing where my Peggy and I kiss and toy.

O! the month of May, the merry month of May,
　So frolic, so gay, and so green, so green, so green!
And then did I unto my true Love say,
　Sweet Peg, thou shalt be my Summer's Queen.

Thomas Dekker (c. 1570–1632)

'Sumer is icumen in'

Sumer is icumen in,
Loud sing cuckoo!
Groweth seed and bloweth mead
And springeth the wood now.
Sing cuckoo!

Ewe bleateth after lamb,
Cow loweth after calf,
Bullock starteth, buck farteth,
Merry sing cuckoo!

Cuckoo, cuckoo!
Well singest thou cuckoo,
Nor cease thou never now!

Sing cuckoo now, sing cuckoo!
Sing cuckoo, sing cuckoo now!

Anon.

The Throstle

'Summer is coming, summer is coming.
    I know it, I know it, I know it.
Light again, leaf again, life again, love again,'
    Yes, my wild little Poet.

Sing the new year in under the blue.
    Last year you sang it as gladly.
'New, new, new, new'! Is it then so new
    That you should carol so madly?

'Love again, song again, nest again, young again,'
    Never a prophet so crazy!
And hardly a daisy as yet, little friend,
    See, there is hardly a daisy.

'Here again, here, here, here, happy year'!
    O warble unchidden, unbidden!
Summer is coming, is coming, my dear,
    And all the winters are hidden.

Alfred, Lord Tennyson (1809–1892)

The Landrail

How sweet and pleasant grows the way
Through summer time again
While Landrails call from day to day
Amid the grass and grain

We hear it in the weeding time
When knee deep waves the corn
We hear it in the summers prime
Through meadows night and morn

And now I hear it in the grass
That grows as sweet again
And let a minutes notice pass
And now tis in the grain

Tis like a fancy every where
A sort of living doubt
We know tis something but it neer
Will blab the secret out

If heard in close or meadow plots
It flies if we pursue
But follows if we notice not
The close and meadow through

Boys know the note of many a bird
In their birdnesting bounds
But when the landrails noise is heard
They wonder at the sounds

They look in every tuft of grass
Thats in their rambles met
They peep in every bush they pass
And none the wiser get

And still they hear the craiking sound
And still they wonder why
It surely cant be under ground
Nor is it in the sky

And yet tis heard in every vale
An undiscovered song
And makes a pleasant wonder tale
For all the summer long

The shepherd whistles through his hands
And starts with many a whoop
His busy dog across the lands
In hopes to fright it up

Tis still a minutes length or more
Till dogs are off and gone
Then sings and louder than before
But keeps the secret on

Yet accident will often meet
The nest within its way
And weeders when they weed the wheat
Discover where they lay

And mowers on the meadow lea
Chance on their noisey guest
And wonder what the bird can be
That lays without a nest

In simple holes that birds will rake
When dusting on the ground
They drop their eggs of curious make
Deep blotched and nearly round

A mystery still to men and boys
Who know not where they lay
And guess it but a summer noise
Among the meadow hay

John Clare (1793–1864)

The Lake Isle of Innisfree

I will arise and go now, and go to Innisfree,
And a small cabin build there, of clay and wattles
    made:
Nine bean-rows will I have there, a hive for the
    honey-bee,
And live alone in the bee-loud glade.

And I shall have some peace there, for peace comes
    dropping slow,
Dropping from the veils of the morning to where the
    cricket sings;
There midnight's all a glimmer, and noon a purple
    glow,
And evening full of the linnet's wings.

I will arise and go now, for always night and day
I hear lake water lapping with low sounds by the
    shore;
While I stand on the roadway, or on the pavements
    grey,
I hear it in the deep heart's core.

W. B. Yeats (1865–1939)

Seven Times One: Exultation

There's no dew left on the daisies and clover,
  There's no rain left in heaven:
I've said my 'seven times' over and over,
  Seven times one are seven.

I am old, so old, I can write a letter;
  My birthday lessons are done;
The lambs play always, they know no better;
  They are only one times one.

O moon! in the night I have seen you sailing
  And shining so round and low.
You were bright! ah bright! but your light is failing –
  You are nothing now but a bow.

You moon! have you done something wrong in heaven
  That God has hidden your face?
I hope if you have you will soon be forgiven,
  And shine again in your place.

O velvet bee, you're a dusty fellow,
  You've powdered your legs with gold!
O brave marsh marybuds, rich and yellow,
  Give me your money to hold!

O columbine, open your folded wrapper,
  Where two twin turtle-doves dwell!
O cuckoopint, toll me the purple clapper
  That hangs in your clear green bell!

And show me your nest with the young ones in it;
  I will not steal them away;
I am old! you may trust me, linnet, linnet –
  I am seven times one today.

Jean Ingelow (1820–1897)

This Lime-tree Bower my Prison

Well, they are gone, and here must I remain,
This lime-tree bower my prison! I have lost
Beauties and feelings, such as would have been
Most sweet to my remembrance even when age
Had dimmed mine eyes to blindness! They,
   meanwhile,
Friends, whom I never more may meet again,
On springy heath, along the hill-top edge,
Wander in gladness, and wind down, perchance,
To that still roaring dell, of which I told;
The roaring dell, o'erwooded, narrow, deep,
And only speckled by the mid-day sun;
Where its slim trunk the ash from rock to rock
Flings arching like a bridge; – that branchless ash,
Unsunned and damp, whose few poor yellow leaves
Ne'er tremble in the gale, yet tremble still,
Fanned by the water-fall! and there my friends
Behold the dark green file of long lank weeds,
That all at once (a most fantastic sight!)
Still nod and drip beneath the dripping edge
Of the blue clay-stone.

           Now, my friends emerge
Beneath the wide wide Heaven – and view again
The many-steepled tract magnificent
Of hilly fields and meadows, and the sea,
With some fair bark, perhaps, whose sails light up
The slip of smooth clear blue betwixt two Isles
Of purple shadow! Yes! they wander on
In gladness all; but thou, methinks, most glad,
My gentle-hearted Charles! for thou hast pined

And hungered after Nature, many a year,
In the great City pent, winning thy way
With sad yet patient soul, through evil and pain
And strange calamity! Ah! slowly sink
Behind the western ridge, thou glorious Sun!
Shine in the slant beams of the sinking orb,
Ye purple heath-flowers! richlier burn, ye clouds!
Live in the yellow light, ye distant groves!
And kindle, thou blue Ocean! So my friend
Struck with deep joy may stand, as I have stood,
Silent with swimming sense; yea, gazing round
On the wide landscape, gaze till all doth seem
Less gross than bodily; and of such hues
As veil the Almighty Spirit, when yet he makes
Spirits perceive his presence.

                A delight
Comes sudden on my heart, and I am glad
As I myself were there! Nor in this bower,
This little lime-tree bower, have I not marked
Much that has soothed me. Pale beneath the blaze
Hung the transparent foliage; and I watched
Some broad and sunny leaf, and loved to see
The shadow of the leaf and stem above
Dappling its sunshine! And that walnut-tree
Was richly tinged, and a deep radiance lay
Full on the ancient ivy, which usurps
Those fronting elms, and now, with blackest mass
Makes their dark branches gleam a lighter hue
Through the late twilight: and though now the bat
Wheels silent by, and not a swallow twitters,
Yet still the solitary humble-bee
Sings in the bean-flower! Henceforth I shall know
That Nature ne'er deserts the wise and pure;

No plot so narrow, be but Nature there,
No waste so vacant, but may well employ
Each faculty of sense, and keep the heart
Awake to Love and Beauty! and sometimes
'Tis well to be bereft of promised good,
That we may lift the soul, and contemplate
With lively joy the joys we cannot share.
My gentle-hearted Charles! when the last rook
Beat its straight path along the dusky air
Homewards, I blest it! deeming its black wing
(Now a dim speck, now vanishing in light)
Had crossed the mighty Orb's dilated glory,
While thou stood'st gazing; or, when all was still,
Flew creeking o'er thy head, and had a charm
For thee, my gentle-hearted Charles, to whom
No sound is dissonant which tells of Life.

Samuel Taylor Coleridge (1772–1834)

The Cow

The friendly cow, all red and white,
I love with all my heart:
She gives me cream with all her might,
To eat with apple-tart.

She wanders lowing here and there,
And yet she cannot stray,
All in the pleasant open air,
The pleasant light of day;

And blown by all the winds that pass
And wet with all the showers,
She walks among the meadow grass
And eats the meadow flowers.

Robert Louis Stevenson (1850–1894)

The Frog

What a wonderful bird the frog are –
When he sit, he stand almost;
When he hop, he fly almost.
He ain't got no sense hardly;
He ain't got no tail hardly either.
When he sit, he sit on what he ain't got – almost.

Anon.

Little Fish

The tiny fish enjoy themselves
in the sea.
Quick little splinters of life,
their little lives are fun to them
in the sea.

D. H. Lawrence (1885–1930)

Heaven

Fish (fly-replete, in depth of June,
Dawdling away their wat'ry noon)
Ponder deep wisdom, dark or clear,
Each secret fishy hope or fear.
Fish say, they have their Stream and Pond;
But is there anything Beyond?
This life cannot be All, they swear,
For how unpleasant, if it were!
One may not doubt that, somehow, Good
Shall come of Water and of Mud;
And, sure, the reverent eye must see
A Purpose in Liquidity.
We darkly know, by Faith we cry,
The future is not Wholly Dry.
Mud unto mud! – Death eddies near –
Not here the appointed End, not here!
But somewhere, beyond Space and Time,
Is wetter water, slimier slime!
And there (they trust) there swimmeth One
Who swam ere rivers were begun,
Immense, of fishy form and mind,
Squamous, omnipotent, and kind;
And under that Almighty Fin,
The littlest fish may enter in.
Oh! never fly conceals a hook,
Fish say, in the Eternal Brook,
But more than mundane weeds are there,
And mud, celestially fair;
Fat caterpillars drift around,
And Paradisal grubs are found;

Unfading moths, immortal flies,
And the worm that never dies.
And in that Heaven of all their wish,
There shall be no more land, say fish.

Rupert Brooke (1887–1915)

To Make a Prairie

To make a prairie it takes a clover and one bee,
One clover, and a bee,
And revery.
The revery alone will do,
If bees are few.

Emily Dickinson (1830–1886)

The Unknown Bird

Three lovely notes he whistled, too soft to be heard
If others sang; but others never sang
In the great beech-wood all that May and June.
No one saw him: I alone could hear him:
Though many listened. Was it but four years
Ago? or five? He never came again.

Oftenest when I heard him I was alone,
Nor could I ever make another hear.
La-la-la! he called, seeming far-off—
As if a cock crowed past the edge of the world,
As if the bird or I were in a dream.
Yet that he travelled through the trees and sometimes
Neared me, was plain, though somehow distant still
He sounded. All the proof is—I told men
What I had heard.

I never knew a voice,
Man, beast, or bird, better than this. I told
The naturalists; but neither had they heard
Anything like the notes that did so haunt me,
I had them clear by heart and have them still.
Four years, or five, have made no difference. Then
As now that La-la-la! was bodiless sweet:
Sad more than joyful it was, if I must say
That it was one or other, but if sad
'Twas sad only with joy too, too far off
For me to taste it. But I cannot tell
If truly never anything but fair
The days were when he sang, as now they seem.

This surely I know, that I who listened then,
Happy sometimes, sometimes suffering
A heavy body and a heavy heart,
Now straightway, if I think of it, become
Light as that bird wandering beyond my shore.

Edward Thomas (1878–1917)

To a Skylark

Hail to thee, blithe Spirit!
Bird thou never wert,
That from heaven or near it,
Pourest thy full heart
In profuse strains of unpremeditated art.

Higher still and higher
From the earth thou springest
Like a cloud of fire;
The blue deep thou wingest,
And singing still doth soar, and soaring every singest.

Percy Bysshe Shelley (1792–1822)

Trees

I think that I shall never see
A poem lovely as a tree.

A tree whose hungry mouth is prest
Against the earth's sweet flowing breast;

A tree that looks at God all day,
And lifts her leafy arms to pray;

A tree that may in summer wear
A nest of robins in her hair;

Upon whose bosom snow has lain;
Who intimately lives with rain.

Poems are made by fools like me
But only God can make a tree.

Joyce Kilmer (1886–1918)

The Sweet o' the Year

Now the frog, all lean and weak,
   Yawning from his famished sleep,
Water in the ditch doth seek,
   Fast as he can stretch and leap:
         Marshy king-cups burning near
         Tell him 'tis the sweet o' the year.

Now the ant works up his mound
   In the mouldered piny soil,
And above the busy ground
   Takes the joy of earnest toil:
         Dropping pine-cones, dry and sere,
         Warn him 'tis the sweet o' the year.

Now the chrysalis on the wall
   Cracks, and out the creature springs,
Raptures in his body small,
   Wonders on his dusty wings:
         Bells and cups, all shining clear,
         Show him 'tis the sweet o' the year.

Now the brown bee, wild and wise,
   Hums abroad, and roves and roams,
Storing in his wealthy thighs
   Treasure for the golden combs:
         Dewy buds and blossoms dear
         Whisper 'tis the sweet o' the year.

Now the merry maids so fair
   Weave the wreaths and choose the queen,
Blooming in the open air,
   Like fresh flowers upon the green;
        Spring, in every thought sincere,
        Thrills them with the sweet o' the year.

Now the lads, all quick and gay,
   Whistle to the browsing herds,
Or in the twilight pastures grey
   Learn the use of whispered words:
        First a blush, and then a tear,
        And then a smile, i' the sweet o' the year.

Now the May-fly and the fish
   Play again from noon to night;
Every breeze begets a wish,
   Every motion means delight:
        Heaven high over heath and mere
        Crowns with blue the sweet o' the year.

Now all Nature is alive,
   Bird and beetle, man and mole;
Bee-like goes the human hive,
   Lark-like sings the soaring soul:
        Hearty faith and honest cheer
        Welcome in the sweet o' the year.

George Meredith (1828–1909)

Ladybird! Ladybird!

Ladybird! Ladybird! Fly away home,
Night is approaching and sunset has come:
The herons are flown to their trees by the Hall;
Felt, but unseen, the damp dewdrops fall.
This is the close of a still summer day;
Ladybird! Ladybird! Haste! fly away!

Emily Brontë (1818–1848)

Daisies

Where innocent bright-eyed daisies are,
With blades of grass between,
Each daisy stands up like a star
Out of a sky of green,

Christina Rossetti (1830–1894)

Where the Bee Sucks

Where the bee sucks, there suck I:
In a cowslip's bell I lie;
There I couch when owls do cry.
On the bat's back I do fly
After summer merrily.
Merrily, merrily shall I live now
Under the blossom that hangs on the bough.

William Shakespeare (1564–1616)

The Gardener

The gardener stood at the garden gate,
  A primrose in his hand;
He saw a lovely girl come by,
  Slim as a willow wand

'O lady, can you fancy me,
  And will you share my life?
All my garden flowers are yours,
  If you will be my wife.

'The white lily will be your shirt
  It suits your body best;
With cornflowers in your hair,
  A red rose on your breast.

'Your gloves will be the marigold,
  Glittering on your hand;
Your dress will be the sweet-william
  That grows upon the bank.'

'Young man, I cannot be your wife;
  I fear it will not do.
Although you care for me,' she said,
  'I cannot care for you.

'As you've provided clothes for me
  Among the summer flowers,
So I'll provide some clothes for you
  Among the winter showers.

'The fallen snow will be your shirt,
    It suits your body best;
Your head will be wound with the eastern wind,
    With the cold rain on your breast.

'Your boots will be of the seaweed
    That drifts upon the tide;
Your horse will be the white wave –
    Leap on, young man, and ride!'

Anon.

The Cries of London

Here's fine rosemary, sage, and thyme.
Come buy my ground ivy.
Here's fetherfew, gilliflowers and rue.
Come buy my knotted marjorum, ho!
Come buy my mint, my fine green mint.
Here's fine lavender for your cloaths.
Here's parsley and winter-savory,
And hearts-ease, which all do choose.
Here's balm and hissop, and cinquefoil,
All fine herbs, it is well known.
    Let none despise the merry, merry cries
    Of famous London-town!

Here's fine herrings, eight a groat.
Hot codlins, pies and tarts.
New mackerel! have to sell.
Come buy my Wellfleet oysters, ho!
Come buy my whitings fine and new.
Wives, shall I mend your husbands horns?
I'll grind your knives to please your wives,
And very nicely cut your corns.
Maids, have you any hair to sell,
Either flaxen, black, or brown?
    Let none despise the merry, merry cries
    Of famous London-town!

Anon.

Scarborough Fair

Where are you going? To Scarborough Fair?
Parsley, sage, rosemary and thyme,
Remember me to a bonny lass there,
For once she was a true lover of mine.

Tell her to make me a cambric shirt,
Parsley, sage, rosemary and thyme,
Without any needle or thread work'd in it,
And she shall be a true lover of mine.

Tell her to wash it in yonder well,
Parsley, sage, rosemary and thyme,
Where water ne'er sprung nor a drop of rain fell,
And she shall be a true lover of mine.

Tell her to plough me an acre of land,
Parsley, sage, rosemary and thyme,
Between the sea and the salt sea strand,
And she shall be a true lover of mine.

Tell her to plough it with one ram's horn,
Parsley, sage, rosemary and thyme,
And sow it all over with one peppercorn,
And she shall be a true lover of mine.

Tell her to reap it with a sickle of leather,
Parsley, sage, rosemary and thyme,
And tie it all up with a tom tit's feather,
And she shall be a true lover of mine.

Tell her to gather it all in a sack,
Parsley, sage, rosemary and thyme,
And carry it home on a butterfly's back,
And then she shall be a true lover of mine.

Anon.

from A Midsummer Night's Dream

I know a bank where the wild thyme blows,
Where oxlips and the nodding violet grows,
Quite over-canopied with luscious woodbine,
With sweet musk-roses and with eglantine:
There sleeps Titania sometime of the night,
Lull'd in these flowers with dances and delight;
And there the snake throws her enamell'd skin,
Weed wide enough to wrap a fairy in:
And with the juice of this I'll streak her eyes,
And make her full of hateful fantasies.
Take thou some of it, and seek through this grove:
A sweet Athenian lady is in love
With a disdainful youth: anoint his eyes;
But do it when the next thing he espies
May be the lady: thou shalt know the man
By the Athenian garments he hath on.
Effect it with some care, that he may prove
More fond on her than she upon her love:
And look thou meet me ere the first cock crow.

William Shakespeare (1564–1616)

Summer Dawn

Pray but one prayer for me 'twixt thy closed lips;
　　Think but one thought of me up in the stars.
The summer night waneth, the morning light slips,
　　Faint and grey 'twixt the leaves of the aspen,
　　　　betwixt the cloud-bars,
That are patiently waiting there for the dawn:
　　Patient and colourless, though Heaven's gold
Waits to float through them along with the sun.
Far out in the meadows, above the young corn,
　　The heavy elms wait, and restless and cold
The uneasy wind rises; the roses are dun;
Through the long twilight they pray for the dawn,
Round the lone house in the midst of the corn.
　　Speak but one word to me over the corn,
　　Over the tender, bowed locks of the corn.

William Morris (1834–1896)

Careless Rambles

I love to wander at my idle will
In summer's luscious prime about the fields
And kneel when thirsty at the little rill
To sip the draught its pebbly bottom yields
And where the maple bush its fountain shields
To lie and rest a swailey hour away
And crop the swelling peascod from the land
Or mid the uplands woodland walks to stray
Where oaks for aye o'er their old shadows stand
Neath whose dark foliage with a welcome hand
I pluck the luscious strawberry ripe and red
As beauty's lips – and in my fancy's dreams
As mid the velvet moss I musing tread
Feel life as lovely as her picture seems.

John Clare (1793–1864)

A Green Cornfield

The earth was green, the sky was blue:
  I saw and heard one sunny morn
A skylark hang between the two,
  A singing speck above the corn;

A stage below, in gay accord,
  White butterflies danced on the wing,
And still the singing skylark soared,
  And silent sank and soared to sing.

The cornfield stretched a tender green
  To right and left beside my walks;
I knew he had a nest unseen
  Somewhere among the million stalks.

And as I paused to hear his song
  While swift the sunny moments slid,
Perhaps his mate sat listening long,
  And listened longer than I did.

Christina Rossetti (1830–1894)

The Caterpillar

Brown and furry
Caterpillar in a hurry,
Take your walk
To the shady leaf, or stalk,
Or what not,
Which may be the chosen spot.
No toad to spy you,
Hovering bird of prey pass by you;
Spin and die,
To live again a butterfly.

Christina Rossetti (1830–1894)

To a Butterfly

I've watched you now a full half-hour,
Self-poised upon that yellow flower;
And, little Butterfly! Indeed
I know not if you sleep or feed.
How motionless! – not frozen seas
Moe motionless! And then
What joy awaits you, when the breeze
Hath found you out among the trees,
And calls you forth again!

This plot of orchard-ground is ours;
My trees they are, my Sister's flowers.
Here rest your wings when they are weary;
Here lodge as in a sanctuary!
Come often to us, fear no wrong;
Sit near us on the bough!
We'll talk of sunshine and of song,
And summer days when we were young;
Sweet childish days, that were as long
As twenty days are now.

William Wordsworth (1770–1850)

Adlestrop

Yes. I remember Adlestrop –
The name, because one afternoon
Of heat the express-train drew up there
Unwontedly. It was late June.

The steam hissed. Someone cleared his throat.
No one left and no one came
On the bare platform. What I saw
Was Adlestrop – only the name

And willows, willow-herb, and grass,
And meadowsweet, and haycocks dry,
No whit less still and lonely fair
Than the high cloudlets in the sky.

And for that minute a blackbird sang
Close by, and round him, mistier,
Farther and farther, all the birds
Of Oxfordshire and Gloucestershire.

Edward Thomas (1878–1917)

Fly Away, Fly Away Over the Sea

Fly away, fly away over the sea,
  Sun-loving swallow, for summer is done;
Come again, come again, come back to me,
  Bringing the summer and bringing the sun.

Christina Rossetti (1830–1894)

Epitaph on a Hare

Here lies, whom hound did ne'er pursue,
Nor swifter greyhound follow,
Whose foot ne'er tainted morning dew,
Nor ear heard huntsman's hallo',

Old Tiney, surliest of his kind,
Who, nursed with tender care,
And to domestic bounds confined,
Was still a wild jack-hare.

Though duly from my hand he took
His pittance every night,
He did it with a jealous look,
And, when he could, would bite.

His diet was of wheaten bread,
And milk, and oats, and straw,
Thistles, or lettuces instead,
With sand to scour his maw.

On twigs of hawthorn he regaled,
On pippins' russet peel;
And, when his juicy salads failed,
Sliced carrot pleased him well.

A Turkey carpet was his lawn,
Whereon he loved to bound,
To skip and gambol like a fawn,
And swing his rump around,

His frisking was at evening hours,
For then he lost his fear;
But most before approaching showers,
Or when a storm drew near.

Eight years and five round-rolling moons
He thus saw steal away,
Dozing out all his idle noons,
And every night at play.

I kept him for his humour's sake,
For he would oft beguile
My heart of thoughts that made it ache,
And force me to a smile.

But now, beneath this walnut-shade
He finds his long, last home,
And waits in snug concealment laid,
Till gentler Puss shall come.

He, still more aged, feels the shocks
From which no care can save,
And, partner once of Tiney's box,
Must soon partake his grave.

William Cowper (1731–1800)

A London Plane-Tree

Green is the plane-tree in the square,
   The other trees are brown;
They droop and pine for country air;
   The plane-tree loves the town.

Here, from my garret-pane, I mark
   The plane-tree bud and blow,
Shed her recuperative bark,
   And spread her shade below.

Among her branches, in and out,
   The city breezes play;
The dun fog wraps her round about;
   Above, the smoke curls grey.

Others the country take for choice,
   And hold the town in scorn;
But she has listened to the voice
   On city breezes borne.

Amy Levy (1861–1889)

In the Fields

Lord, when I look at lovely things which pass,
  Under old trees the shadows of young leaves
Dancing to please the wind along the grass,
  Or the gold stillness of the August sun on the
    August sheaves;
Can I believe there is a heavenlier world than this?
  And if there is
Will the strange heart of any everlasting thing
  Bring me these dreams that take my breath away?
They come at evening with the home-flying rooks and
    the scent of hay,
  Over the fields. They come in Spring.

Charlotte Mew (1869–1928)

Meeting at Night

The grey sea and the long black land;
And the yellow half-moon large and low;
And the startled little waves that leap
In fiery ringlets from their sleep,
As I gain the cove with pushing prow,
And quench its speed i' the slushy sand.

Then a mile of warm sea-scented beach;
Three fields to cross till a farm appears;
A tap at the pane, the quick sharp scratch
And blue spurt of a lighted match,
And a voice less loud, thro' its joys and fears,
Than the two hearts beating each to each!

Robert Browning (1812–1889)

AUTUMN

To Autumn

Season of mists and mellow fruitfulness,
  Close bosom-friend of the maturing sun;
Conspiring with him how to load and bless
  With fruit the vines that round the thatch-eves run;
To bend with apples the moss'd cottage-trees,
  And fill all fruit with ripeness to the core;
    To swell the gourd, and plump the hazel shells
  With a sweet kernel; to set budding more,
And still more, later flowers for the bees,
Until they think warm days will never cease,
    For summer has o'er-brimm'd their clammy cells.

Who hath not seen thee oft amid thy store?
  Sometimes whoever seeks abroad may find
Thee sitting careless on a granary floor,
  Thy hair soft-lifted by the winnowing wind;
Or on a half-reap'd furrow sound asleep,
  Drows'd with the fume of poppies, while thy hook
    Spares the next swath and all its twined flowers:
And sometimes like a gleaner thou dost keep
  Steady thy laden head across a brook;
Or by a cyder-press, with patient look,
  Thou watchest the last oozings hours by hours.

Where are the songs of Spring? Ay, where are they?
  Think not of them, thou hast thy music too,—
While barred clouds bloom the soft-dying day,
  And touch the stubble-plains with rosy hue;
Then in a wailful choir the small gnats mourn
  Among the river sallows, borne aloft
    Or sinking as the light wind lives or dies;
And full-grown lambs loud bleat from hilly bourn;
  Hedge-crickets sing; and now with treble soft
  The red-breast whistles from a garden-croft;
    And gathering swallows twitter in the skies.

John Keats (1795–1821)

Leisure

What is this life if, full of care,
We have no time to stand and stare?—

No time to stand beneath the boughs,
And stare as long as sheep or cows:

No time to see, when woods we pass,
Where squirrels hide their nuts in grass:

No time to see, in broad daylight,
Streams full of stars, like skies at night:

No time to turn at Beauty's glance,
And watch her feet, how they can dance:

No time to wait till her mouth can
Enrich that smile her eyes began?

A poor life this if, full of care,
We have no time to stand and stare.

W. H. Davies (1871–1940)

from Give me the Splendid, Silent Sun

Give me the splendid silent sun, with all his beams
    full-dazzling;
Give me juicy autumnal fruit, ripe and red from the
    orchard;
Give me a field where the unmow'd grass grows;
Give me an arbor, give me the trellis'd grape;
Give me fresh corn and wheat—give me serene-
    moving animals, teaching content;
Give me nights perfectly quiet, as on high plateaus
    west of the Mississippi, and I looking up at the
    stars;
Give me odorous at sunrise a garden of beautiful
    flowers, where I can walk undisturb'd;
Give me for marriage a sweet-breath'd woman, of
    whom I should never tire;
Give me a perfect child—give me, away, aside from
    the noise of the world, a rural, domestic life;
Give me to warble spontaneous songs, reliev'd, recluse
    by myself, for my own ears only;
Give me solitude—give me Nature—give me again,
    O Nature, your primal sanities!

Walt Whitman (1819–1892)

Pied Beauty

Glory be to God for dappled things –
    For skies of couple-colour as a brinded cow;
      For rose-moles all in stipple upon trout that
        swim;
Fresh-firecoal chestnut-falls; finches' wings;
    Landscape plotted and pieced – fold, fallow,
        and plough;
      And all trades, their gear and tackle and trim.

All things counter, original, spare, strange;
    Whatever is fickle, freckled (who knows how?)
      With swift, slow; sweet, sour; adazzle, dim;
He fathers-forth whose beauty is past change:
                    Praise him.

Gerard Manley Hopkins (1844–1889)

The Glory

The glory of the beauty of the morning, –
The cuckoo crying over the untouched dew;
The blackbird that has found it, and the dove
That tempts me on to something sweeter than love;
White clouds ranged even and fair as new-mown hay;
The heat, the stir, the sublime vacancy
Of sky and meadow and forest and my own heart: –
The glory invites me, yet it leaves me scorning
All I can ever do, all I can be,
Beside the lovely of motion, shape, and hue,
The happiness I fancy fit to dwell
In beauty's presence. Shall I now this day
Begin to seek as far as heaven, as hell,
Wisdom or strength to match this beauty, start
And tread the pale dust pitted with small dark drops,
In hope to find whatever it is I seek,
Hearkening to short-lived happy-seeming things
That we know naught of, in the hazel copse?
Or must I be content with discontent
As larks and swallows are perhaps with wings?
And shall I ask at the day's end once more
What beauty is, and what I can have meant
By happiness? And shall I let all go,
Glad, weary, or both? Or shall I perhaps know
That I was happy oft and oft before,
Awhile forgetting how I am fast pent,
How dreary-swift, with naught to travel to,
Is Time? I cannot bite the day to the core.

Edward Thomas (1878–1917)

The Rainy Day

The day is cold, and dark, and dreary;
It rains, and the wind is never weary;
The vine still clings to the mouldering wall,
But at every gust the dead leaves fall,
  And the day is dark and dreary.

My life is cold, and dark, and dreary;
It rains, and the wind is never weary;
My thoughts still cling to the mouldering Past,
But the hopes of youth fall thick in the blast,
  And the days are dark and dreary.

Be still, sad heart! and cease repining;
Behind the clouds is the sun still shining;
Thy fate is the common fate of all,
Into each life some rain must fall,
  Some days must be dark and dreary.

Henry Wadsworth Longfellow (1807–1882)

Autumn Rain

The plane leaves
fall black and wet
on the lawn;

the cloud sheaves
in heaven's fields set
droop and are drawn

in falling seeds of rain;
the seed of heaven
on my face

falling – I hear again
like echoes even
that softly pace

heaven's muffled floor,
the winds that tread
out all the grain

of tears, the store
harvested
in the sheaves of pain

caught up aloft:
the sheaves of dead
men that are slain

now winnowed soft
on the floor of heaven;
manna invisible

of all the pain
here to us given;
finely divisible
falling as rain.

D. H. Lawrence
(1885–1930)

Digging

Today I think
Only with scents, – scents dead leaves yield,
And bracken, and wild carrot's seed,
And the square mustard field;

Odours that rise
When the spade wounds the roots of tree,
Rose, currant, raspberry, or goutweed,
Rhubarb or celery;

The smoke's smell, too,
Flowing from where a bonfire burns
The dead, the waste, the dangerous,
And all to sweetness turns.

It is enough
To smell, to crumble the dark earth,
While the robin sings over again
Sad songs of Autumn mirth.

Edward Thomas (1878–1917)

Autumn Fires

In the other gardens
  And all up the vale,
From the autumn bonfires
  See the smoke trail!

Pleasant summer over
  And all the summer flowers,
The red fire blazes,
  The grey smoke towers.

Sing a song of seasons!
  Something bright in all!
Flowers in the summer,
  Fires in the fall!

Robert Louis Stevenson
(1850–1894)

Now is the Time for the Burning of the Leaves

Now is the time for the burning of the leaves.
They go to the fire; the nostril pricks with smoke
Wandering slowly into a weeping mist.
Brittle and blotched, ragged and rotten sheaves!
A flame seizes the smouldering ruin and bites
On stubborn stalks that crackle as they resist.

The last hollyhock's fallen tower is dust;
All the spices of June are a bitter reek,
All the extravagant riches spent and mean.
All burns! The reddest rose is a ghost;
Sparks whirl up, to expire in the mist: the wild
Fingers of fire are making corruption clean.

Now is the time for stripping the spirit bare,
Time for the burning of days ended and done,
Idle solace of things that have gone before:
Rootless hope and fruitless desire are there;
Let them go to the fire, with never a look behind.
The world that was ours is a world that is ours no
   more.

They will come again, the leaf and the flower, to arise
From squalor of rottenness into the old splendour,
And magical scents to a wondering memory bring;
The same glory, to shine upon different eyes.
Earth cares for her own ruins, naught for ours.
Nothing is certain, only the certain spring.

Laurence Binyon (1869–1943)

Moonlit Apples

At the top of the house the apples are laid in rows,
And the skylight lets the moonlight in, and those
Apples are deep-sea apples of green. There goes
   A cloud on the moon in the autumn night.

A mouse in the wainscot scratches, and scratches, and
     then
There is no sound at the top of the house of men
Or mice; and the cloud is blown, and the moon again
   Dapples the apples with deep-sea light.

They are lying in rows there, under the gloomy beams;
On the sagging floor; they gather the silver streams
Out of the moon, those moonlit apples of dreams,
   And quiet is the steep stair under.

In the corridors under there is nothing but sleep.
And stiller than ever on orchard boughs they keep
Tryst with the moon, and deep is the silence, deep
   On moon-washed apples of wonder.

John Drinkwater (1882–1937)

The Lane

Some day, I think, there will be people enough
In Froxfield to pick all the blackberries
Out of the hedges of Green Lane, the straight
Broad lane where now September hides herself
In bracken and blackberry, harebell and dwarf gorse.
Today, where yesterday a hundred sheep
Were nibbling, halcyon bells shake to the sway
Of waters that no vessel ever sailed . . .
It is a kind of spring: the chaffinch tries
His song. For heat it is like summer too.
This might be winter's quiet. While the glint
Of hollies dark in the swollen hedges lasts—
One mile—and those bells ring, little I know
Or heed if time be still the same, until
The lane ends and once more all is the same.

Edward Thomas (1878–1917)

The Wild Swans at Coole

The trees are in their autumn beauty,
The woodland paths are dry,
Under the October twilight the water
Mirrors a still sky;
Upon the brimming water among the stones
Are nine-and-fifty swans.

The nineteenth autumn has come upon me
Since I first made my count;
I saw, before I had well finished,
All suddenly mount
And scatter wheeling in great broken rings
Upon their clamorous wings.

I have looked upon those brilliant creatures,
And now my heart is sore.
All's changed since I, hearing at twilight,
The first time on this shore,
The bell-beat of their wings above my head,
Trod with a lighter tread.

Unwearied still, lover by lover,
They paddle in the cold
Companionable streams or climb the air;
Their hearts have not grown old;
Passion or conquest, wander where they will,
Attend upon them still.

But now they drift on the still water,
Mysterious, beautiful;
Among what rushes will they build,
By what lake's edge or pool
Delight men's eyes when I awake some day
To find they have flown away?

W. B. Yeats (1865–1939)

'Western wind, when wilt thou blow?'

Western wind, when wilt thou blow,
The small rain down can rain?
Christ, if my love were in my arms
And I in my bed again.

Anon.

Who Has Seen the Wind?

Who has seen the wind?
  Neither I nor you:
But when the leaves hang trembling,
  The wind is passing thro'.

Who has seen the wind?
  Neither you nor I:
But when the trees bow down their heads,
  The wind is passing by.

Christina Rossetti (1830–1894)

from The Garden

What wondrous life in this I lead!
Ripe apples drop about my head;
The luscious clusters of the vine
Upon my mouth do crush their wine;
The nectarine, and curious peach,
Into my hands themselves do reach;
Stumbling on melons, as I pass,
Ensnared with flowers, I fall on grass.

Meanwhile the mind, from pleasure less,
Withdraws into its happiness:
The mind, that ocean where each kind
Does straight its own resemblance find;
Yet it creates, transcending these,
Far other worlds, and other seas;
Annihilating all that's made
To a green thought in a green shade.

Andrew Marvell (1621–1678)

Autumn Birds

The wild duck startles like a sudden thought,
And heron slows as if it might be caught;
The flopping crows on weary wings go by,
And greybeard jackdaws, noising as they fly;
The crowds of starlings whizz and hurry by
And darken like a cloud the evening sky;
The larks like thunder rise and suther round
Then drop and nest in the stubble ground;
The wild swan hurries high and noises loud,
With white neck peering to the evening cloud.
The weary rooks to distant woods are gone;
With length of tail the magpie winnows on
To neighbouring tree, and leaves the distant crow,
While small birds nestle in the hedge below.

John Clare (1793–1864)

The Windhover

To Christ Our Lord

I caught this morning morning's minion, kingdom of
  daylight's dauphin, dapple-dawn-drawn Falcon, in
    his riding
  Of the rolling level underneath him steady air,
    and striding
High there, how he rung upon the rein of a wimpling
  wing
In his ecstasy! then off, off forth on swing,
  As a skate's heel sweeps smooth on a bow-bend:
    the hurl and gliding
  Rebuffed the big wind. My heart in hiding
Stirred for a bird, – the achieve of, the mastery of the
  thing.

Brute beauty and valour and act, oh, air, pride,
  Plume, here
  Buckle! AND the fire that breaks from thee
    then, a billion
Times told lovelier, more dangerous, O my chevalier!

  No wonder of it: shéer plód makes plough down
    sillion
Shine, and blue-bleak embers, ah my dear,
  Fall, gall themselves, and gash gold-vermilion.

Gerard Manley Hopkins (1844–1889)

The Owl

*Of all the night's creatures, the owl has
perhaps the most evocative cry.*

When cats run home and light is come,
  And dew is cold upon the ground,
And the far-off stream is dumb,
  And the whirring sail goes round,
  And the whirring sail goes round;
    Alone and warming his five wits,
    The white owl in the belfry sits.

When merry milkmaids click the latch,
  And rarely smells the new-mown hay,
And the cock hath sung beneath the thatch
  Twice or thrice his roundelay,
  Twice or thrice his roundelay;
    Alone and warming his five wits,
    The white owl in the belfry sits.

Alfred, Lord Tennyson (1809–1892)

Sweet Suffolke Owle

Sweet Suffolke Owle, so trimly dight,
With feathers like a Lady bright,
Thou sing'st alone, sitting, by night,
   Te whit, te whoo,
Thy note that forth so freely roules,
With shrill command the Mouse controules,
And sings a dirge for dying soules,
   Te whit, te whoo.

Anon.

Rural Evening

The whip cracks on the plough-team's flank,
   The thresher's flail beats duller.
The round of day has warmed a bank
   Of cloud to primrose colour.

The dairy girls cry home the kine,
   The kine in answer lowing;
And rough-haired louts with sleepy shouts
   Keep crows whence seed is growing.

The creaking wain, brushed through the lane
   Hangs straws on hedges narrow;
And smoothly cleaves the soughing plough,
   And harsher grinds the harrow.

Comes, from the road-side inn caught up,
   A brawl of crowded laughter,
Thro' falling brooks and cawing rooks
   And a fiddle scrambling after.

Lord De Tabley (1835–1895)

The Hayloft

Through all the pleasant meadow-side
  The grass grew shoulder-high,
Till the shining scythes went far and wide
  And cut it down to dry.

These green and sweetly smelling crops
  They led in wagons home;
And they piled them here in mountain tops
  For mountaineers to roam.

Here is Mount Clear, Mount Rusty-Nail,
  Mount Eagle and Mount High –
The mice that in these mountains dwell,
  No happier are than I!

O what a joy to clamber there,
  O what a place for play,
With the sweet, the dim, the dusty air,
  The happy hills of hay!

Robert Louis Stevenson (1850–1894)

The Solitary Reaper

Behold her, single in the field,
Yon solitary Highland Lass!
Reaping and singing by herself;
Stop here, or gently pass!
Alone she cuts and binds the grain,
And sings a melancholy strain;
O listen! for the Vale profound
Is overflowing with the sound.

No Nightingale did ever chaunt
More welcome notes to weary bands
Of travellers in some shady haunt,
Among Arabian sands:
A voice so thrilling ne'er was heard
In spring-time from the Cuckoo-bird,
Breaking the silence of the seas
Among the farthest Hebrides.

Will no one tell me what she sings?
Perhaps the plaintive numbers flow
For old, unhappy, far-off things,
And battles long ago:
Or is it some more humble lay,
Familiar matter of today?
Some natural sorrow, loss, or pain,
That has been, and may be again?

Whate'er the theme, the Maiden sang
As if her song could have no ending;
I saw her singing at her work,
And o'er the sickle bending;—
I listened, motionless and still;
And, as I mounted up the hill,
The music in my heart I bore,
Long after it was heard no more.

William Wordsworth (1770–1850)

To a Squirrel at Kyle-Na-No

Come play with me;
Why should you run
Through the shaking tree
As though I'd a gun
To strike you dead?
When all I would do
Is to scratch your head
And let you go.

W. B. Yeats (1865–1939)

The Way through the Woods

They shut the road through the woods
Seventy years ago.
Weather and rain have undone it again,
And now you would never know
There was once a road through the woods
Before they planted the trees.
It is underneath the coppice and heath,
And the thin anemones.
Only the keeper sees
That, where the ring-dove broods,
And the badgers roll at ease,
There was once a road through the woods.

Rudyard Kipling (1865–1936)

The Fisherman's Wife

When I am alone,
The wind in the pine-trees
Is like the shuffling of waves
Upon the wooden sides of a boat.

Amy Lowell (1874–1925)

Signs of the Times

Air a-gittin' cool an' coolah,
  Frost a-comin' in de night,
Hicka' nuts an' wa'nuts fallin',
  Possum keepin' out o' sight.
Tu'key struttin' in de ba'nya'd,
  Nary step so proud ez his;
Keep on struttin', Mistah Tu'key,
  Yo' do' know whut time it is.

Cidah press commence a-squeakin'
  Eatin' apples sto'ed away,
Chillun swa'min' 'roun' lak ho'nets,
  Huntin' aigs ermung de hay.
Mistah Tu'key keep on gobblin'
  At de geese a-flyin' souf,
Oomph! dat bird do' know whut's comin';
  Ef he did he'd shet his mouf.

Pumpkin gittin' good an' yallah
  Mek me open up my eyes;
Seems lak it's a-lookin' at me
  Jes' a-la'in' dah sayin' 'Pies.'
Tu'key gobbler gwine 'roun' blowin',
  Gwine 'roun' gibbin' sass an' slack;
Keep on talkin', Mistah Tu'key,
  You ain't seed no almanac.

Fa'mer walkin' th'oo de ba'nya'd
  Seein' how things is comin' on,
Sees ef all de fowls is fatt'nin' –
  Good times comin' sho's you bo'n.

Hyeahs dat tu'key gobbler braggin',
  Den his face break in a smile –
Nebbah min', you sassy rascal,
  He's gwine nab you atter while.

Choppin' suet in de kitchen,
  Stonin' raisins in de hall,
Beef a-cookin' fu' de mince meat,
  Spices groun' – I smell 'em all.
Look hyeah, Tu'key, stop dat gobblin',
  You ain' luned de sense ob feah,
You ol' fool, yo' naik's in dangah,
  Do' you know Thanksgibbin's hyeah?

Paul Laurence Dunbar (1876–1906)

Fall, Leaves, Fall

Fall, leaves, fall; die, flowers, away;
Lengthen night and shorten day;
Every leaf speaks bliss to me
Fluttering from the autumn tree.
I shall smile when wreaths of snow
Blossom where the rose should grow;
I shall sing when night's decay
Ushers in a drearier day.

Emily Brontë (1818–1848)

Pleasant Sounds

The rustling of leaves under the feet in woods and
  under hedges;
The crumping of cat-ice and snow down wood-rides,
  narrow lanes, and every street causeway;
Rustling through a wood or rather rushing, while the
  wind halloos in the oak-toop like thunder;
The rustle of birds' wings startled from their nests or
  flying unseen into the bushes;
The whizzing of larger birds overhead in a wood, such
  as crows, puddocks, buzzards;
The trample of robins and woodlarks on the brown
  leaves, and the patter of squirrels on the green
  moss;
The fall of an acorn on the ground, the pattering of
  nuts on the hazel branches as they fall from
  ripeness;
The flirt of the groundlark's wing from the stubbles –
  how sweet such pictures on dewy mornings, when
  the dew flashes from its brown feathers.

John Clare (1793–1864)

A Noiseless, Patient Spider

A noiseless, patient spider,
I marked, where, on a little promontory, it stood
   isolated;
Marked how, to explore the vacant, vast surrounding,
It launched forth filament, filament, filament, out of
   itself;
Ever unreeling them – ever tirelessly speeding them.

And you, O my Soul, where you stand,
Surrounded, surrounded, in measureless oceans of
   space,
Ceaselessly musing, venturing, throwing, – seeking the
   spheres, to connect them;
Till the bridge you will need, be formed – till the
   ductile anchor hold;
Till the gossamer thread you fling, catch somewhere,
   O my Soul.

Walt Whitman (1819–1892)

Something Told the Wild Geese

Something told the wild geese
   It was time to go.
Though the fields lay golden
   Something whispered, – 'Snow.'

Leaves were green and stirring,
   Berries, lustre-glossed,
But beneath warm feathers
   Something cautioned, – 'Frost.'

All the sagging orchards
   Steamed with amber spice,
But each wild breast stiffened
   At remembered Ice.

Something told the wild geese
   It was time to fly, –
Summer sun was on their wings,
   Winter in their cry.

Rachel Field (1894–1942)

WINTER

To a Mouse

On turning Her up in her Nest with
the Plough, November 1785

Wee, sleeket, cowran, tim'rous beastie,
O, what a panic's in thy breastie!
Thou need na start awa sae hasty,
    Wi' bickerin brattle!
I wad be laith to rin an' chase thee
    Wi' murd'ring pattle!

I'm truly sorry Man's dominion
Has broken Nature's social union,
An' justifies that ill opinion,
    Which makes thee startle,
At me, thy poor, earth-born companion,
    An' fellow-mortal!

I doubt na, whyles, but thou may thieve;
What then? poor beastie, thou maun live!
A daimen-icker in a thrave
    'S a sma' request:
I'll get a blessin wi' the lave,
    An' never miss 't!

Thy wee-bit housie, too, in ruin!
It's silly wa's the win's are strewin!
An' naething, now, to big a new ane,
    O' foggage green!
An' bleak December's winds ensuin,
    Baith snell an' keen!

Thou saw the fields laid bare an' waste,
An' weary Winter comin fast,
An' cozie here, beneath the blast,
    Thou thought to dwell,
Till crash! the cruel coulter past
      Out thro' thy cell.

That wee-bit heap o' leaves an' stibble
Has cost thee monie a weary nibble!
Now thou's turn'd out, for a' thy trouble,
    But house or hald,
To thole the Winter's sleety dribble,
      An' cranreuch cauld!

But Mousie, thou art no thy-lane,
In proving foresight may be vain:
The best laid schemes o' Mice an' Men
    Gang aft agley,
An' lea'e us nought but grief an' pain,
      For promis'd joy!

Still, thou art blest, compar'd wi' me!
The present only toucheth thee:
But Och! I backward cast my e'e,
    On prospects drear!
An' forward tho' I canna see,
      I guess an' fear!

Robert Burns (1759–1796)

Spellbound

The night is darkening round me,
The wild winds coldly blow;
But a tyrant spell has bound me
And I cannot, cannot go.

The giant trees are bending
Their bare boughs weighed with snow.
And the storm is fast descending,
And yet I cannot go.

Clouds beyond clouds above me,
Wastes beyond wastes below;
But nothing drear can move me;
I will not, cannot go.

Emily Brontë (1818–1848)

Winter-Time

Late lies the wintry sun a-bed,
A frosty, fiery sleepy-head;
Blinks but an hour or two; and then,
A blood-red orange, sets again.

Before the stars have left the skies,
At morning in the dark I rise;
And shivering in my nakedness,
By the cold candle, bathe and dress.

Close by the jolly fire I sit
To warm my frozen bones a bit;
Or with a reindeer-sled, explore
The colder countries round the door.

When to go out, my nurse doth wrap
Me in my comforter and cap;
The cold wind burns my face, and blows
Its frosty pepper up my nose.

Black are my steps on silver sod;
Thick blows my frosty breath abroad;
And tree and house, and hill and lake,
Are frosted like a wedding cake.

Robert Louis Stevenson (1850–1894)

Winter

The boughs, the boughs are bare enough
But earth has never felt the snow.
Frost-furred our ivies are, and rough

With bills of rime the brambles shew.
The hoarse leaves crawl on hissing ground
Because the sighing wind is low.

But if the rain-blasts be unbound
And from dank feathers wring the drops
The clogged brook runs with choking sound

Kneading the mounded mire that stops
His channel under damming coats
Of foliage fallen in the copse.

A simple passage of weak notes
Is all the winter bird dare try
The bugle moon by daylight floats

So glassy white about the sky,
So like a berg of hyaline,
And pencilled blue so daintily,

I never saw her so divine
But through black branches, rarely drest
In scarves of silky shot and shine.

The webbèd and the watery west
Where yonder crimson fireball sits
Looks laid for feasting and for rest.

I see long reefs of violets
In beryl-covered fens so dim,
A gold-water Pactolus frets

Its brindled wharves and yellow brim,
The waxen colours weep and run
And slendering to his burning rim

Into the flat blue mist the sun
Drops out and all our day is done.

Gerard Manley Hopkins (1844–1889)

A Winter Night

It was a chilly winter's night;
  And frost was glitt'ring on the ground,
And evening stars were twinkling bright;
  And from the gloomy plain around
    Came no sound,
But where, within the wood-girt tow'r,
The churchbell slowly struck the hour;

As if that all of human birth
  Had risen to the final day,
And soaring from the wornout earth
  Were called in hurry and dismay,
    Far away;
And I alone of all mankind
Were left in loneliness behind.

William Barnes (1801–1886)

Snow Storm

What a night! The wind howls, hisses, and but stops
To howl more loud, while the snow volley keeps
Incessant batter at the window pane,
Making our comfort feel as sweet again;
And in the morning, when the tempest drops,
At every cottage door mountainous heaps
Of snow lie drifted, that all entrance stops
Until the beesom and the shovel gain
The path, and leave a wall on either side.
The shepherd rambling valleys white and wide
With new sensations his old memory fills,
When hedges left at night, no more described,
Are turned to one white sweep of curving hills,
And trees turned bushes half their bodies hide.

The boy that goes to fodder with surprise
Walks oer the gate he opened yesternight.
The hedges all have vanished from his eyes;
Een some tree tops the sheep could reach to bite.
The novel scene emboldens new delight,
And, though with cautious steps his sports begin,
He bolder shuffles the huge hills of snow,
Till down he drops and plunges to the chin,
And struggles much and oft escape to win –
Then turns and laughs but dare not further go;
For deep the grass and bushes lie below,
Where little birds that soon at eve went in
With heads tucked in their wings now pine for day
And little feel boys oer their heads can stray.

John Clare (1793–1864)

No!

No sun – no moon!
No morn – no noon!
No dawn – no dusk – no proper time of day –
No sky – no earthly view –
No distance looking blue –
No road – no street – no 't'other side this way' –
No end to any Row –
No indications where the Crescents go –
No top to any steeple –
No recognitions of familiar people –
No courtesies for showing 'em –
No knowing 'em!
No travelling at all – no locomotion –
No inkling of the way – no notion –
'No go' by land or ocean –
No mail – no post –
No news from any foreign coast –
No Park, no Ring, no afternoon gentility –
No company – no nobility –
No warmth, no cheerfulness, no healthful ease,
No comfortable feel in any member –
No shade, no shine, no butterflies, no bees,
No fruits, no flowers, no leaves, no birds –
November!

Thomas Hood (1799–1845)

Sheep in Winter

The sheep get up and make their many tracks
And bear a load of snow upon their backs,
And gnaw the frozen turnip to the ground
With sharp quick bite, and then go noising round
The boy that pecks the turnips all the day
And knocks his hands to keep the cold away
And laps his legs in straw to keep them warm
And hides behind the hedges from the storm.
The sheep, as tame as dogs, go where he goes
And try to shake their fleeces from the snows,
Then leave their frozen meal and wander round
The stubble stack that stands beside the ground,
And lie all night and face the drizzling storm
And shun the hovel where they might be warm.

John Clare (1793–1864)

Snow

In the gloom of whiteness,
In the great silence of snow,
A child was sighing
And bitterly saying: 'Oh,
They have killed a white bird up there on her nest,
The down is fluttering from her breast!'
And still it fell through the dusky brightness
On the child crying for the bird of the snow.

Edward Thomas (1878–1917)

Out in the Dark

Out in the dark over the snow
The fallow fawns invisible go
With the fallow doe;
And the winds blow
Fast as the stars are slow.

Stealthily the dark haunts round
And, when the lamp goes, without sound
At a swifter bound
Than the swiftest hound,
Arrives, and all else is drowned;

And star and I and wind and deer,
Are in the dark together, – near,
Yet far, – and fear
Drums on my ear
In the sage company drear.

How weak and little is the light,
All the universe of sight,
Love and delight,
Before the might,
If you love it not, of night.

Edward Thomas (1878–1917)

The Fallow Deer at the Lonely House

One without looks in tonight
   Through the curtain-chink
From the sheet of glistening white;
One without looks in tonight
   As we sit and think
   By the fender-brink.

We do not discern those eyes
   Watching in the snow;
Lit by lamps of rosy dyes
We do not discern those eyes
   Wondering, aglow,
   Fourfooted, tiptoe.

Thomas Hardy (1840–1928)

from As You Like It

Blow, blow, thou winter wind,
  Thou art not so unkind
    As man's ingratitude;
  Thy tooth is not so keen,
Because thou art not seen,
    Although thy breath be rude.
Heigh-ho! sing, heigh-ho! unto the green holly:
Most friendship is feigning, most loving mere folly:
  Then, heigh-ho, the holly!
    This life is most jolly.

  Freeze, freeze, thou bitter sky,
  That dost not bite so nigh
    As benefits forgot:
  Though thou the waters warp,
    Thy sting is not so sharp
    As friend remembered not.
Heigh-ho! sing, heigh-ho! unto the green holly . . .
Most friendship is feigning, most loving mere folly:
  Then, heigh-ho, the holly!
    This life is most jolly.

William Shakespeare (1564–1616)

A Winter Bluejay

Crisply the bright snow whispered,
Crunching beneath our feet;
Behind us as we walked along the parkway,
Our shadows danced
Fantastic shapes in vivid blue.
Across the lake the skaters
Flew to and fro,
With sharp turns weaving
A frail invisible net.
In ecstasy the earth
Drank the silver sunlight;
In ecstasy the skaters
Drank the wine of speed;
In ecstasy we laughed
Drinking the wine of love.
Had not the music of our joy
Sounded its highest note?
But no,
For suddenly, with lifted eyes you said,
'Oh look!'
There, on the black bough of a snow-flecked maple,
Fearless and gay as our love,
A bluejay cocked his crest!
Oh, who can tell the range of joy
Or set the bounds of beauty?

Sara Teasdale (1884–1933)

Birds at Winter Nightfall

Around the house the flakes fly faster,
And all the berries now are gone
From holly and cotoneaster
Around the house. The flakes fly! faster
Shutting indoors that crumb-outcaster
We used to see upon the lawn
Around the house. The flakes fly faster,
And all the berries now are gone!

Thomas Hardy (1840–1928)

The Darkling Thrush

I leant upon a coppice gate
    When Frost was spectre-grey,
And Winter's dregs made desolate
    The weakening eye of day.
The tangled bine-stems scored the sky
    Like strings of broken lyres,
And all mankind that haunted nigh
    Had sought their household fires.

The land's sharp features seemed to be
    The Century's corpse outleant,
His crypt the cloudy canopy,
    The wind his death-lament.
The ancient pulse of germ and birth
    Was shrunken hard and dry,
And every spirit upon earth
    Seemed fervourless as I.

At once a voice arose among
    The bleak twigs overhead
In a full-hearted evensong
    Of joy illimited;
An aged thrush, frail, gaunt, and small,
    In blast-beruffled plume,
Had chosen thus to fling his soul
    Upon the growing gloom.

Thomas Hardy (1840–1928)

Little Robin Redbreast

Little Robin Redbreast
Sat upon a tree,
He sang merrily,
As merrily as could be.
He nodded with his head,
And his tail waggled he,
As little Robin Redbreast
Sat upon a tree.

Anon.

Frost at Midnight

The Frost performs its secret ministry,
Unhelped by any wind. The owlet's cry
Came loud—and hark, again! loud as before.
The inmates of my cottage, all at rest,
Have left me to that solitude, which suits
Abstruser musings: save that at my side
My cradled infant slumbers peacefully.
'Tis calm indeed! so calm, that it disturbs
And vexes meditation with its strange
And extreme silentness. Sea, hill, and wood,
This populous village! Sea, and hill, and wood,
With all the numberless goings-on of life,
Inaudible as dreams! the thin blue flame
Lies on my low-burnt fire, and quivers not;
Only that film, which fluttered on the grate,
Still flutters there, the sole unquiet thing.
Methinks, its motion in this hush of nature
Gives it dim sympathies with me who live,
Making it a companionable form,
Whose puny flaps and freaks the idling Spirit
By its own moods interprets, every where
Echo or mirror seeking of itself,
And makes a toy of Thought.

                        But O! how oft,
How oft, at school, with most believing mind,
Presageful, have I gazed upon the bars,
To watch that fluttering stranger! and as oft
With unclosed lids, already had I dreamt
Of my sweet birthplace, and the old church tower,
Whose bells, the poor man's only music, rang

From morn to evening, all the hot Fair-day,
So sweetly, that they stirred and haunted me
With a wild pleasure, falling on mine ear
Most like articulate sounds of things to come!
So gazed I, till the soothing things, I dreamt,
Lulled me to sleep, and sleep prolonged my dreams!
And so I brooded all the following morn,
Awed by the stern preceptor's face, mine eye
Fixed with mock study on my swimming book:
Save if the door half opened, and I snatched
A hasty glance, and still my heart leaped up,
For still I hoped to see the stranger's face,
Townsman, or aunt, or sister more beloved,
My playmate when we both were clothed alike!

   Dear Babe, that sleepest cradled by my side,
Whose gentle breathings, heard in this deep calm,
Fill up the interspersèd vacancies
And momentary pauses of the thought!
My babe so beautiful! it thrills my heart
With tender gladness, thus to look at thee,
And think that thou shalt learn far other lore,
And in far other scenes! For I was reared
In the great city, pent 'mid cloisters dim,
And saw nought lovely but the sky and stars.
But thou, my babe! shalt wander like a breeze
By lakes and sandy shores, beneath the crags
Of ancient mountain, and beneath the clouds,
Which image in their bulk both lakes and shores
And mountain crags: so shalt thou see and hear
The lovely shapes and sounds intelligible
Of that eternal language, which thy God
Utters, who from eternity doth teach
Himself in all, and all things in himself.

Great universal Teacher! he shall mould
Thy spirit, and by giving make it ask.

    Therefore all seasons shall be sweet to thee,
Whether the summer clothe the general earth
With greenness, or the redbreast sit and sing
Betwixt the tufts of snow on the bare branch
Of mossy apple tree, while the nigh thatch
Smokes in the sun-thaw; whether the eave-drops fall
Heard only in the trances of the blast,
Or if the secret ministry of frost
Shall hang them up in silent icicles,
Quietly shining to the quiet Moon.

Samuel Taylor Coleridge (1772–1834)

Up in the Morning Early

Cauld blaws the wind frae east to west,
　The drift is driving sairly;
Sae loud and shrill's I hear the blast,
　I'm sure it's winter fairly.

CHORUS: Up in the morning's no for me,
　Up in the morning early;
When a' the hills are cover'd wi' snaw,
　I'm sure it's winter fairly.

The birds sit chittering in the thorn,
　A' day they fare but sparely;
And lang's the night frae e'en to morn,
　I'm sure it's winter fairly.

CHORUS: Up in the morning's no for me,
　Up in the morning early;
When a' the hills are cover'd wi' snaw,
　I'm sure it's winter fairly.

Robert Burns (1759–1796)

In Tenebris

All within is warm,
  Here without it's very cold,
  Now the year is grown so old
And the dead leaves swarm.

In your heart is light,
  Here without it's very dark,
  When shall I hear the lark?
When see aright?

Oh, for a moment's space!
  Draw the clinging curtains wide
  Whilst I wait and yearn outside
Let the light fall on my face.

Ford Madox Ford (1873–1939)

The Holly and the Ivy

The holly and the ivy,
When they are both full grown,
Of all the trees that are in the wood,
The holly bears the crown.

The rising of the sun
And the running of the deer,
The playing of the merry organ,
Sweet singing in the choir.

The holly bears a blossom
As white as the lily flower,
And Mary bore sweet Jesus Christ
To be our sweet Savour.

The holly bears a berry
As red as any blood,
And Mary bore sweet Jesus Christ
To do poor sinners good.

The holly bears a prickle
As sharp as any thorn,
And Mary bore sweet Jesus Christ
On Christmas Day in the morn.

The holly bears a bark
As bitter as any gall,
And Mary bore sweet Jesus Christ
For to redeem us all.

The holly and the ivy,
When they are both full grown,
Of all the trees that are in the wood,
The holly bears the crown.

Anon.

The First Tree in the Greenwood

Now the holly bears a berry as white as the milk,
And Mary bore Jesus, who was wrapped up in silk:
And Mary bore Jesus Christ,
Our Saviour for to be,
And the first tree in the greenwood, it was the holly.

Now the holly bears a berry as green as the grass,
And Mary bore Jesus, who died on the cross:
And Mary bore Jesus Christ,
Our Saviour for to be,
And the first tree in the greenwood, it was the holly.

Now the holly bears a berry as black as the coal,
And Mary bore Jesus, who died for us all:
And Mary bore Jesus Christ,
Our Saviour for to be,
And the first tree in the greenwood, it was the holly.

Now the holly bears a berry, as blood is it red,
Then trust we our Saviour, who rose from the dead:
And Mary bore Jesus Christ,
Our Saviour for to be,
And the first tree in the greenwood, it was the holly.

Anon.

The Oxen

Christmas Eve, and twelve of the clock.
'Now they are all on their knees,'
An elder said as we sat in a flock
By the embers in hearthside ease.

We pictured the meek mild creatures where
They dwelt in their strawy pen
Nor did it occur to one of us there
To doubt they were kneeling then.

So fair a fancy few would weave
In these years! Yet, I feel,
If someone said on Christmas Eve,
'Come; see the oxen kneel

'In the lonely barton by yonder coomb
Our childhood used to know,'
I should go with him in the gloom,
Hoping it might be so.

Thomas Hardy (1840–1928)

Index of Poets

Index of Titles

Index of First Lines

MACMILLAN COLLECTOR'S LIBRARY

Own the world's great works of literature in one beautiful collectible library

Designed and curated to appeal to book lovers everywhere, Macmillan Collector's Library editions are small enough to travel with you and striking enough to take pride of place on your bookshelf. These much-loved literary classics also make the perfect gift.

Beautifully produced with gilt edges, a ribbon marker, bespoke illustrated cover and real cloth binding, every Macmillan Collector's Library hardback adheres to the same high production values.

Discover something new or cherish your favourite stories with this elegant collection.

Macmillan Collector's Library: own, collect, and treasure

Discover the full range at
macmillancollectorslibrary.com